CONTENTS

KT-511-313

A potent icon

One of the internationally recognised icons of the Scottish Highlands, the Glenfinnan Monument is set in some of the most romantic and inspiring scenery in Scotland. It stands on low ground at the head of Loch Shiel, with the hills of Ardgour, Moidart and Lochaber rising dramatically around it, and its framing by the surrounding landscape gives it enormous visual power.

Yet it is far more than simply an eye-catching monument. It also functions as a symbol of the Jacobite Rising of 1745, an attempt to restore the Stuarts to the British throne in place of the reigning Hanoverian monarchy. The Rising, led by Prince Charles Edward Stuart – 'Bonnie Prince Charlie' – began at Glenfinnan, where the Prince first mustered support, but ended in disastrous failure less than a year later. This defeat led to the imposition of draconian measures by the British government to suppress any further rebellions by the Highland clans, and hastened massive changes in the social organisation and culture of the Scottish Highlands.

The Monument serves as a memorial to these dramatic events in Scottish history, whose impact was felt far beyond the shores of Britain. The building was completed in 1815 and embellished in the 1830s, less than a century after the events it commemorated and the harsh repression that followed. After the Rising was crushed, the kilted Highlander was identified by the Hanoverian government with Jacobitism, political treachery and opposition to the monarchy. A raft of legislation outlawed Highland dress, tartan and other clan traditions. But later in the eighteenth century, during Britain's wars of empire, Highland soldiers in the British army were allowed to wear tartan. This began the gradual rehabilitation of the Gael and, within a generation, the transformation from villain to hero was complete. Nowhere is this more graphically demonstrated than in the Glenfinnan Monument, whose statue shows a stereotypical Highlander figure imbued with virtues of courage, gallantry and loyalty, surrounded by a rugged, Romantic landscape.

An inscribed marble panel, which was previously above the doorway but is now set into the perimeter wall, describes how the tower commemorates not only Bonnie Prince Charlie and the Highlanders killed in the Jacobite conflicts, but also Alexander Macdonald of Glenaladale, the local landowner who had the Monument built, and

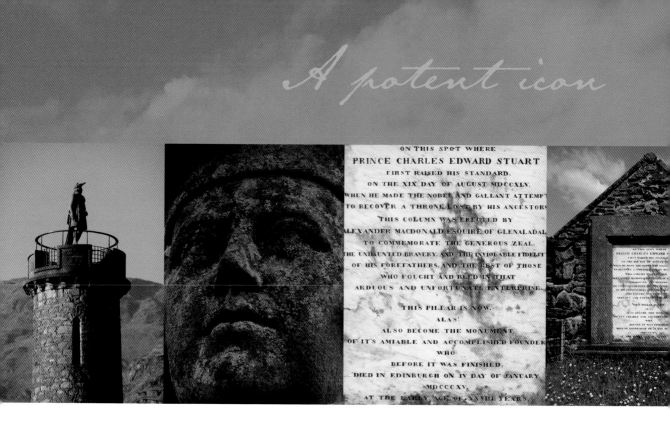

ON THIS SPOT WHERE
PRINCE CHARLES EDWARD STUART
FIRST RAISED HIS STANDARD,
ON THE XIX DAY OF AUGUST MDCCXLV,
WHEN HE MADE THE NOBLE AND GALLANT ATTEMPT
TO RECOVER A THRONE LOST BY HIS ANCESTORS
THIS COLUMN WAS ERECTED BY
ALEXANDER MACDONALD ESQUIRE OF GLENALADALE
TO COMMEMORATE THE GENEROUS ZEAL,
THE UNDAUNTED BRAVERY, AND THE INVIOLABLE FIDELITY
OF HIS FOREFATHERS, AND THE REST OF THOSE
WHO FOUGHT AND BLED IN THAT
ARDUOUS AND UNFORTUNATE ENTERPRISE.

THIS PILLAR IS NOW
ALAS!
ALSO BECOME THE MONUMENT
OF IT'S AMIABLE AND ACCOMPLISHED FOUNDER
WHO
BEFORE IT WAS FINISHED,
DIED IN EDINBURGH ON IV DAY OF JANUARY
MDCCCXV,
AT THE EARLY AGE OF XXVIII YEARS

who died at an early age the year it was completed. Glenaladale's father was the cousin of the clan chief with whom the Prince had lodged the night before his Standard was raised at Glenfinnan, and who fought with him throughout the Rising. The inscription reads:

'On this spot Prince Charles Edward Stuart raised his Standard on the XIX day of August MDCCXLV when he made his daring and romantic attempt to recover a throne lost by the imprudence of his ancestors. This column was erected by Alexander Macdonald, Esquire, of Glenaladale, to commemorate the generous zeal, and the inviolable fidelity of his forefathers, and to the rest of those who fought and bled in that arduous and unfortunate enterprise. This pillar is now alas! also become the monument of its amiable and accomplished founder who, before it was finished, died in Edinburgh on the IV day of January MDCCCXV at the early age of XXVIII years.'

The Monument was transferred to the ownership of the National Trust for Scotland in 1938. It was donated by Sir Walter Blount on behalf of himself, Glenaladale Estates and the Roman Catholic Diocese of Argyll and the Isles. The surrounding land is protected by a Conservation Agreement, preventing alteration to the property without the Trust's agreement.

The Jacobite cause

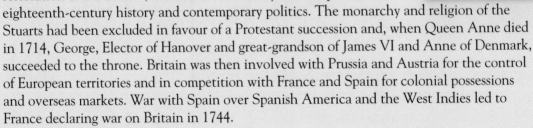

The Raising of the Standard at Glenfinnan on 19 August 1745 marked the effective beginning of the military attempt to restore the Stuarts to the British throne. James VII of Scotland and II of England (left), the grandfather of Prince Charles Edward, had been forced out of Britain in what became known as the 'Glorious Revolution'. His insistence on the Divine Right of kings and freedom of worship for fellow Roman Catholics led to his being deposed from the throne in 1688 and to the Scottish parliament, in turn, deciding in 1689 that James had forfeited his right to the kingship. The Protestant William of Orange and his wife Mary, James's daughter, were then offered the crown as joint sovereigns.

Those who continued to support the Stuarts' claim to the throne were termed 'Jacobites', from the Latin *Jacobus* (James). They upheld the political principles of Divine Right and irreversible hereditary succession; rejected the Glorious Revolution; and opposed the Act of Union, objecting to Scotland's diminished status in the United Kingdom after 1707. They secretly and openly planned an invasion by the exiled Stuarts with foreign help, and invasion expeditions were launched in 1708, 1715 and 1719. Though many people in Scotland and England might have preferred a return of the Stuarts, few believed as late as the 1740s that the cause had any real prospect of success. There was certainly a widening discrepancy between those who might drink toasts to 'the king over the water' and those who would still be prepared to take up arms in the Stuarts' cause.

Viewed in hindsight, the Rising of 1745 takes on the gloss of romance, adventure and tragedy – or it can be dismissed as absolute folly. Neither of these interpretations does justice to the issue of the restoration of the Stuarts, which was clouded by the complexities of eighteenth-century history and contemporary politics. The monarchy and religion of the Stuarts had been excluded in favour of a Protestant succession and, when Queen Anne died in 1714, George, Elector of Hanover and great-grandson of James VI and Anne of Denmark, succeeded to the throne. Britain was then involved with Prussia and Austria for the control of European territories and in competition with France and Spain for colonial possessions and overseas markets. War with Spain over Spanish America and the West Indies led to France declaring war on Britain in 1744.

The support of France was the key to Jacobite success – but it was forthcoming only when it contributed directly to the French cause. Charles had been secretly invited to Paris by Louis XV in late 1743 and an invasion of Britain became a real prospect when France and Britain were at war the following year. The plan was for the Prince to accompany a French invasion fleet of 10,000 men then gathering in the Channel ports, land at Maldon on the Essex coast, and march at the head of Jacobite troops to claim London and the throne. Charles had gained the impression that the French king would endorse his regency in the name of James, his father.

But the French ships and troop transports were scattered by storms in March 1744. The forces were redirected to land operations in Flanders, culminating in a French victory over British troops commanded by the Duke of Cumberland at the Battle of Fontenoy on 30 April 1745. The expectations among Jacobite exiles of substantial French support were never met, and Jacobites were not prepared to undertake military action without the prospect of a French invasion. Although dislike of the Hanoverian regime and Jacobite sympathy was certainly widespread, it did not cause the people of Britain to take up arms.

'Bonnie Prince Charlie'

Prince Charles Edward Stuart was born in Rome on 31 December 1720. His mother was Clementina Sobieska (1702-35), granddaughter of the King of Poland. His father was the exiled Stuart, James VIII of Scotland and III of England, proclaimed king after the death of his father in 1701, and consequently referred to as 'The Pretender' by those who opposed a Stuart restoration. The birth of a son and heir to the Stuarts in exile, who was given the title of the Prince of Wales, reinvigorated the political cause of the Jacobites. A second son, Henry Benedict, was born on 6 March 1725 and given the title of Duke of York.

The children were brought up at the Stuart court in the Muti Palace in Rome. The Prince was 'Carluccio' to his father, who was half Italian and had spent most of his life on the Continent. The court itself was a hub of European intrigue, a little world of rumour, bickering and fantasy. Reports to the court in exile of the strength of Jacobitism in England and Scotland were consistently exaggerated. Charles Edward, who had inherited his mother's high spirits and quick temper rather than his father's moody, reserved character, grew up with a fierce ambition to win back Britain for King James VIII and III.

The Baptism of Prince Charles Edward Stuart at the Muti Palace, Rome, by Antonio David, 1725. Opposite page: portrait of James VII and II by Nicolas de Largillière, 1685; Jacobite drinking glass engraved with a portrait of Prince Charles Edward Stuart

The Prince comes 'home' to Scotland

By mid-1745 Prince Charles, believing that Jacobites in Britain were waiting eagerly for him to lead them into battle, had grown impatient waiting for orders from the French that never came. He set off for Scotland against his father's wishes and the best advice offered, that is, unless he was to come at the head of a French army, he should not come at all. He hired two ships, the *Elisabeth* and the *Du Teillay*, commanded by the Franco-Irish shipowner and privateer, Antoine Walsh, and his little squadron sailed out of Nantes on 22 June 1745.

In the place of an expected military force and to the intense disappointment and dismay of Scottish Jacobites, Prince Charles Edward had only a small band of companions on the *Du Teillay*, including the so-called 'Seven Men of Moidart'. They were Sir Thomas Sheridan, by then old and infirm, having been the Prince's 'under-governor' since the age of four; Colonel John William O'Sullivan, an Irishman in the French army; William Murray, Marquis of Tullibardine, crippled with rheumatism and living in exile, having lost his title as 'Duke of Atholl' to his brother for his part in the 1715 Rising; Sir John MacDonald, an elderly cavalry officer in the service of France; Francis Strickland, an English Jacobite and member of James's court in Rome; Parson George Kelly, an Irish Episcopalian clergyman; and Aeneas MacDonald, banker in Paris and brother of MacDonald of Kinlochmoidart.

A chance encounter and sea battle with a British warship, *Lion*, badly damaged the larger, sixty-gun *Elisabeth*, carrying arms and ammunition and a company of French marines, and forced her to return to Brest. The *Du Teillay* continued alone and made

landfall in Barra and Eriskay on 23 July, where the Prince intended to make contact with the Outer Isles clan chieftains, in clan territory controlled by MacDonald of Clanranald. The Prince was rebuffed at his first meeting, with Clanranald's brother Alexander MacDonald of Boisdale, who told the Prince bluntly that he must return home, affirming that not a single chief of any

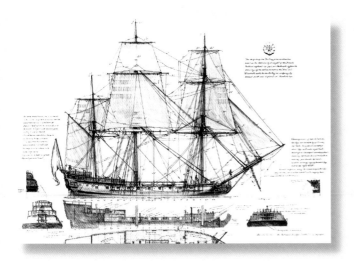

note would be fool enough to support him. The retort from the astonished Prince was: 'I am come home, Sir, and I will entertain no notion at all of returning to that place whence I came, for that I am persuaded my faithful Highlanders will stand by me.'

The *Du Teillay* continued across the Minch and anchored in Loch nan Uamh in Arisaig on St James's Day, 25 July 1745. The news of the Prince's landing did not reach Edinburgh until 8 August and Fort William on 9 August. The government responded by sending troops west to strengthen the garrison in Fort William. Reinforcements included two companies of the Royal Scots who were ambushed at the High Bridge in Lochaber on 16 August by a small band of Highlanders under Donald MacDonell of Tiendrish. The news that Prince Charles Edward had sailed to Scotland had reached London too and on 1 August the British government announced a reward of £30,000 to anyone who seized him.

A caricature of Prince Charles Edward Stuart on a government poster of 1745 offering a £30,000 reward for his capture. Top left: a reconstruction of the French ship Du Teillay, *which carried the Prince to Scotland. Opposite page:* Action at Sea, 9 July 1745, *a painting by Harold Wylie*

While the *Du Teillay* lay at anchor, Prince Charles Edward held court and wrote letters to potential supporters. Some of these have survived: the example below was written to the Earl of Cromarty from Borrodale on 8 August:

> 'Having been well informed of your principles and loyalty, I cannot but expect your assistance at this juncture, that I am come with a firm resolution to restore the King, my father, or perish in the attempt. I know the interest you have among those of your name, and depend on you to exert it to the utmost of your power. … I intend to set up the Royal Standard at Glenfinnan on Monday the 19th instant, and should be very glad to see you on that occasion. If time does not allow it, I still depend upon your joining me with all convenient speed. In the mean time you may be assured of the particular esteem and friendship I have for you.
>
> Charles, P. R.'

Prince Charles Edward taking leave of Antoine Walsh at Loch nan Uamh, by an unknown artist, c1745. The Prince is giving Walsh letters for his father, James. Bottom: portrait of Donald Cameron of Lochiel by an unknown artist, c1745

Early visitors included Ranald MacDonald of Clanranald, Donald MacDonald of Kinlochmoidart and Alexander MacDonald of Glenaladale (ancestor of the future patron of the Monument). These were the leading men of the 'Rough Bounds', or eastern edge of the Clanranald territories. All who came, though feeling duty bound to support the Prince, expressed doubts about the wisdom of what he was proposing and claimed that only French arms could make an invasion succeed. Among those who refused to join the Rising at this juncture without French support were key figures such as MacLeod of MacLeod and MacDonald of Sleat.

However, the Prince refused to bow to pressure, and among many of his supporters a strong sense of honour overcame their better judgement. Ronald, younger brother of MacDonald of Kinlochmoidart, on being challenged by the Prince 'Will you not assist me?' made the fateful response: 'I will! I will! Though no other man in the Highlands should draw a sword, I am ready to die for you.' Donald Cameron of Lochiel, known as the 'Gentle Lochiel' and described by Sir Walter Scott as 'the most amiable and accomplished of the Jacobite heroes', was a central figure in the Prince's plans, and was also forced to overcome his reluctance. A 'Memoir' of Lochiel's recently discovered in Paris opens with the words: 'After making fruitless attempts to persuade HRH to go back to where he came from, Lochiel was in the end alarmed at the dangerous position in which His Royal Person was placed, and brought out nine hundred of his clan.'

The Raising of the Standard

The stores were landed and Antoine Walsh sailed his ship away. After spending some days at Kinlochmoidart, the Prince and his supporters took to boats at Dalilea to go up Loch Shiel, stopping in Glenaladale for the night. They arrived at Glenfinnan about one o'clock in the afternoon on 19 August 1745. The Prince was concerned at first to find no clan army waiting for him but, about three o'clock, Lochiel arrived with 600 or more men. About six o'clock, MacDonald of Keppoch came over the hill with about 350 clansmen and the captured 'redcoats' from High Bridge. With Lochiel's men and about 150 of the Prince's Clanranald supporters under MacDonald of Morar, the Standard was raised before the final contingent came into the glen.

The ceremony was a dramatic and symbolic act. The 'Royal Standard' was a large banner of red silk with a white area in the middle, and was described as 'about twice the size of an ordinary pair of colours'. It was unfurled and held by the Marquis of Tullibardine ('Duke William'). Local Moidart tradition adds that the Standard was sewn by the ladies of Dalilea, the pole was made by a Corbett from Moidart, and Tullibardine was helped to hold the Standard by Aeneas or Duncan MacMaster of Glenaladale and by a Macphee.

Top: a nineteenth-century engraving of the Raising of the Standard; below, a contemporary sketch of the Marquis of Tullibardine

Raising the Standard in Glenfinnan

THE MARQUIS OF TULLIBARDINE

The declaration, dated at Rome, 23 December 1743, was read by Tullibardine and proclaimed the Prince's father, James VIII, as King of England, Scotland and Ireland. Next, a commission was read in the name of his father, appointing Charles, Prince of Wales, to be prince regent. Finally, a manifesto by the Prince himself was read, dated at Paris, 16 May 1745, declaring that he was now come to execute the will of his father by setting up the Royal Standard, asserting the latter's undoubted right to the throne of his ancestors and offering pardon to those who would take up arms on his behalf, or, at the least, abjure allegiance to the usurper. The Highlanders threw their bonnets in the air and cheered, shouting 'Long Live King James the Eighth and Charles Prince of Wales, Prosperity to Scotland and No Union.'

The testimony of the rocks

The commemorative marble tablet at the Monument claims the site as the 'spot where Prince Charles Edward Stuart first raised his Standard'. However, evidence of eye-witness accounts differed in detail, and in 1988 a more likely site was revealed. A hill fire uncovered flat expanses of rock on which inscriptions were carved, indicating that the ceremony of the Standard and gathering of the clans took place on the hill about 300 metres to the north of the Monument, on a raised area above the Glenfinnan church and presbytery. We can still read: 'MDCCXLV In Nomine Domini ...' in Latin, to be translated approximately as '1745, In the Name of the Lord, here the Standards of Charles Edward Stuart, triumphing at last, were set up.' Footprints also are carved, indicating, we suppose, the stance of the Marquis of Tullibardine and of the socket of the Standard, of the Prince and of Bishop Hugh MacDonald, Vicar Apostolic of the Highlands, who blessed the Standard.

Victory and defeat

Following the Raising of the Standard, on 21 August the Prince led his army east by Kinlochiel into Lochaber. General Sir John Cope moved a government force rapidly into the Highlands to oppose him but, finding the Prince's army stronger than he expected, moved back from the Corrieyairack Pass to Inverness. The Prince reached Perth, where he was joined by a number of other clan contingents from the Stewarts of Appin, Glengarry and MacDonalds of Glencoe, and leading men such as James Drummond, Duke of Perth, and Tullibardine's brother, Lord George Murray. The latter was a career soldier, tough and experienced, and was appointed Major-General of the Jacobite army. His straightforward and uncompromising manner did not endear him to the Prince's circle of whom he was generally critical.

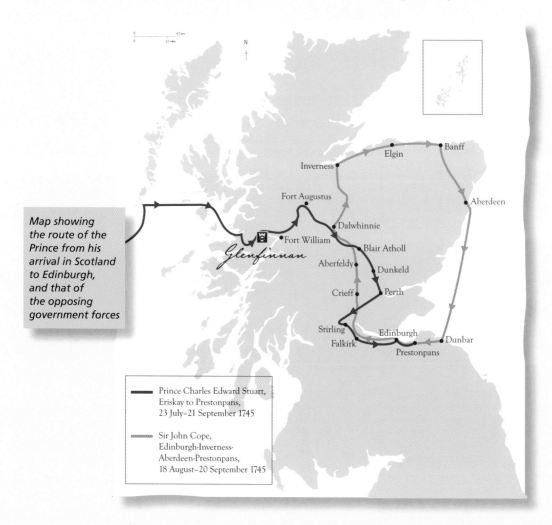

Map showing the route of the Prince from his arrival in Scotland to Edinburgh, and that of the opposing government forces

Prince Charles Edward Stuart,
Eriskay to Prestonpans,
23 July–21 September 1745

Sir John Cope,
Edinburgh-Inverness-
Aberdeen-Prestonpans,
18 August–20 September 1745

A Race from Preston Pans to Berwick.

St John he Bought him an Ambling Nag, / To Scotland for to ride, A, / A hundred horse besides his own, / Did guard him on each side, A, / The Ladies all run to their Windows to see, / So noble & gallant a fight, A,

And as he rode by, they all did Cry, / St John why will you go fight, A, / But still ye Crosell Knigt rode on, / His heart would not relent, A, / For till he came there, he felt no fear, / Why then should he repent, A,

St JOHN SUCK–LYNN, a Bolled. / None liked him so well, as his own Collanel, / He took him for John De Wort, A. / But when they made shews of Gunning & Blows / St John he was nothing so pert, A.

For when the Scots army came in fight, / And all prepar'd to fight, A, / He ran to his tent, & they sli'd o'the ment / Be laid he must needs go an l——, A. / His Collanel sent for him Back again, / To place him in the Van, A.

But St John he did swear, he came not there, / To be kill'd the very first man, A, / To cure him of fear, he was sent to ye rear, / Some five or six miles or more, A. / St John he did play, try trip & away, / And nere see the Enemy more, A.

The army crossed the Forth near Stirling, unopposed, and entered Edinburgh on 17 September. James VIII was proclaimed at the Mercat Cross. Cope, who had marched and shipped his forces from Inverness to Dunbar, advanced towards Edinburgh but was attacked and decisively routed by the Jacobite army at Prestonpans at dawn on 21 September 1745. The Prince was for an immediate advance into England, expecting a sympathetic rising there to draw a French invasion, but his clan leaders had to be persuaded of the strategic importance of the plan. On a west coast route, looking to the Jacobites of Lancashire and Wales to join them, the Prince's army reached Derby on 4 December.

Portrait of Lord George Murray by an unknown artist (c1740). Top: a contemporary cartoon satirising General Cope's flight after his defeat by the Jacobites at Prestonpans

On 6 December 1745, 'Black Friday', to the bitter disappointment of Prince Charles Edward and many of his supporters, the Jacobite army abandoned its plan to march on London, and turned around to return to Scotland. Joining up with considerable reinforcements raised mainly in north-east Scotland, they defeated government forces at Falkirk on 16 January 1746 and then moved north into the Highlands in a last bid to consolidate their position and await French forces, arms and money. Fewer than 1,000 French troops came, late in the day, to help the Prince's cause. On 16 April 1746 on Culloden Moor, a depleted and starved Jacobite army faced a government force, superior in numbers and firepower, under the command of the Duke of Cumberland. The subsequent defeat and rout of the Prince's army was followed by a savage campaign of reprisals and suppression, then by an army of occupation in the Highlands and legislation designed to destroy the clans. The Prince himself was a fugitive in the Highlands and Islands from April, often in desperate straits and hemmed in by cordons of troops, until taken off at Loch nan Uamh in a French ship in September. A few supporters sheltered him and helped him to evade capture. None of them attempted to claim the £30,000 reward for handing him over to the government.

Returning to Paris, Prince Charles Edward enjoyed the attention of an admiring public but failed to gain material support from the Court. He was expelled from France under the terms of the Treaty of Aix-la-Chapelle in 1748, the political turn of events together with the French defeats of 1759 that eclipsed any real hope of winning the throne for his father, who remained the king in exile. The Prince entered a further tragic phase of his life, wandering, more often in disguise, between Switzerland, Germany, the Netherlands and France, and even visiting England secretly in 1750. James, the 'Old Pretender', died on 1 January 1766 but Bonnie Prince Charlie remained a pawn in the complicated game of European power-politics. In his frustration and bitterness, he turned increasingly to heavy drinking and became an embarrassment in political and social circles. The Prince died in Rome without legitimate heirs in 1788. With the death of his brother, Henry Benedict, Cardinal York, in 1807, a direct line of succession to the Stuart family died out.

Portrait of Prince Charles Edward in Rome, 1775, by Hugh Douglas Hamilton. Opposite page, top: An Incident in the Rebellion of 1745 by David Morier; below, a plaque at Loch nan Uamh commemorating Prince Charles' hopeful arrival and bitter departure from Scotland

Prince Charles Edward Stuart: a life in portraits

Prince Charles had little knowledge and no experience of Scotland until the momentous events of 1745-6. His upbringing in Rome is reflected in his early portraits, which at first glance seem merely to show a young Italian nobleman. Indeed there are only two clues in these portraits to associate the Prince with either Scotland or England. He is shown with the Cross of St Andrew, in the jewel of the Scottish Order of the Thistle, suspended from a green ribbon worn around his neck. And he is shown with the blue riband of the English Order of the Garter (**image 1**).

Engravings of these early portraits were made in Paris and widely circulated in Scotland and England. But it was politically dangerous to own them, so the Thistle and the Garter were both omitted. This ensured anonymity, allowing the owner of the engravings, if questioned by the Hanoverian authorities, to deny that they showed the exiled Stuart prince.

As Prince Charles grew older the Stuart Court in Rome contained fewer and fewer Scots (only ten out of 126 people by 1737), and when he was painted full-length by Louis-Gabriel Blanchet (1705-72) at the end of that year the green ribbon and the Thistle jewel were not included. Blanchet's portrait, now in the National Portrait Gallery in London, shows him with the Garter only (**2**).

1

3

2

This apparently exclusive identification with England worried the Scottish Jacobites. In 1738, and again in 1740, the Duke of Perth presented Prince Charles with a Highland costume of tartan, and a volume of Scottish country dances, to stimulate his interest in Scotland. The gift had the desired effect. A version of Blanchet's portrait by William Mosman (c1700-71), probably painted in 1740, shows Prince Charles wearing his new red tartan coat, with a blue bonnet and white cockade on his head (**3**). When Prince Charles was in Paris in 1744-5, waiting to sail for Scotland, he made sure that his new engraved portraits, based on a painting by Domenico Duprà (1689-1770), all showed him with the Thistle prominently displayed with the Garter (**4**).

The months that Prince Charles spent in Scotland had an important influence on his iconography. Although he continued to be portrayed as a European prince, in the conventional aristocratic costume of the day, an alternative tradition emerged in which he was represented as a Scottish national folk hero wearing tartan. The former group of portraits includes the engraving by Robert Strange (1721-92), made while the Prince was at Holyrood, and the various images produced after his return to Paris, notably the pastel by Maurice Quentin de la Tour (1702-88), which is now in the Scottish National Portrait Gallery (**5**). The latter group, often by unidentified artists, includes various copies of the engraving by Robert Strange, but with the Prince dressed in tartan. The so-called 'Harlequin' portraits also belong to this group. The tartan in all of them was a constant reminder of the stirring events of the 1745 Rising.

4

5

The changing image of the Prince: 1) by Antonio David, 1729; 2) by Louis-Gabriel Blanchet, 1737-8; 3) by William Mosman (after Blanchet), c1740; 4) by Domenico Duprà, 1740; 5) by Maurice Quentin de la Tour, 1748

Of particular interest are two anonymous paintings which show Prince Charles on the shore of Loch nan Uamh after his arrival in July 1745, saying farewell to Antoine Walsh. The pictures, though very different, both depict the Prince wearing a tartan kilt, and handing over a letter for Walsh to send on to King James in Rome (**6**). In the distance, as you can see in the reproduction on page 11, Walsh's ship, the *Du Teillay*, lies at anchor in the Sound of Arisaig.

The inspiration for the 'Harlequin' portraits was a painting by E Gill (d 1749), who had previously worked for the Stuart court in Rome. It shows Prince Charles again standing on the northern shore of Loch nan Uamh, with the 'Seven Men of Moidart' in the background (**7**). This time he is wearing a tartan suit, with full-length trews rather than a kilt. His coat is lined with ermine, he has a plaid over his shoulder, and he wears a blue bonnet with a white feather. He has neither the Garter nor the Thistle, but the costume underlines the feeling of identification that the Prince now had with Scotland.

There are many 'Harlequin' portraits, perhaps all painted by James Worsdale (1692-1767). They show Prince Charles wearing half-length tartan breeches, a tartan coat, and a blue bonnet with a white rose. He stands beside the sea in the Hebrides, at some point during the five months he spent in hiding after the Battle of Culloden. The portraits differ slightly in detail, but the striking thing about them is that, although they all show Prince Charles with the Order of the Garter, none of them shows him with the Order of the Thistle (**8**). The costume is evidently now sufficient to establish the close association between the Prince and his father's 'ancient Kingdom'.

6

8

7

After he succeeded his father as the Jacobite king-in-exile, Prince Charles commissioned a formal state portrait from Laurent Pecheux (1729-1821). It was painted in Rome, and shows him in armour as 'King of Great Britain, France and Ireland', with both the Garter and the Thistle. Charles instructed the painter that the background should show the Battle of Prestonpans, and ordered him to add the following inscription (translated here from the original Latin): 'Leaving Edinburgh, the Scottish capital which he had taken, he obtained victory with great courage and triumphed against the enemy in his own country in October 1745'(**9**). The date of the battle fell in October according to the Gregorian, or New Style, calendar used in Roman Catholic Europe, and gradually adopted worldwide. Britain was still using the Julian, or Old Style, calendar, so Prestonpans was (and still is) recorded as having taken place in September 1745.

When this portrait was painted in 1770, and displayed in the Palazzo Stuart in Rome, Prince Charles was in fact a defeated and broken man, no longer the glamorous prince who had inspired so many Scots and whose exploits had made him the most admired man in Europe. Yet the portrait reveals the sense of pride that he still took in the achievements of 1745, and of his continued attachment to the country which, from faraway Rome, he continued to regard as his own.

The changing image of the Prince: 6) by an unknown artist, c1745; 7) by E Gill, c1746-9; 8) by James Worsdale, c1745-6; 9) by Laurent Pecheux, 1770

9

The patron of the Glenfinnan Monument

The Monument to the Jacobite campaign of 1745-6 was commissioned by the local landowner, Alexander Macdonald of Glenaladale, whose father's cousin had supported Prince Charles Edward Stuart. Glenaladale died in 1815, the same year the Monument was completed, at the age of only 28, after a life of excess and reckless consumption.

It is rare to be able to reconstruct the life of a historical character in the detail that is possible with Macdonald. Legal documents in the National Archives of Scotland contain an extraordinary amount of personal information about him. By the time of his death he was in serious debt, owing over 80 different people a total of some £32,000 – perhaps equivalent to over £4,000,000 today. Many of his debts remained uncleared more than ten years after his death, despite the selling off of part of the family estate and the renunciation by his family of some of Macdonald's assets.

Macdonald emerges from the documents as a highly flamboyant character with an instinct for the grand gesture – someone who lived a prodigal, unfettered existence. In this he was very like his own clan chieftain and close friend, Macdonald of Clanranald, who dissipated his inheritance in high living and gambling in London. In fact, Macdonald bought an island and other estate land from Clanranald – perhaps out of a sense of clan loyalty – thus contributing substantially to his own debt.

In 1813 Bishop John Chisholm of Lismore, to whom Macdonald owed over £2000, wrote to him of his reputation as 'a rake and one head and ears in debt'. Following a 'jaunt' to the Hebrides with Clanranald, which the Bishop said 'did not increase your good name', he was encouraged to 'wash away past stains and secure ... the grace and protection of your Creator for the remainder of your temporal existence.'

One of his largest debts was to his solicitors, to whom he owed as much as £377 3s 10d at the time of his death. The list of creditors also shows that his own employees were often left unpaid. His housekeeper, Mrs Margaret Macdonald, was owed £122 14s 5d, and a servant-maid, Betty Cameron, was due £21 17s. Two shepherds at Glenaladale, Angus and Alexander Macdougald, were due £63 and £23 respectively, while a ploughman, John Livingston, was owed £20, and a 'gardner', Robert Mackay, £40.

Yet Macdonald had a generous side and sought to provide credit of £10 with a Glasgow merchant on behalf of a Mrs McGregor, whose husband had died in a drowning accident. He was also celebrated locally in Gaelic poetry of the time, being the subject of a lament published after his death which refers to him poignantly as 'the head of the revered family/Who will be lingering in Edinburgh/In his winter-house and without the power of moving', and to his raising 'a stone and a tower ... That were as memorials of gloom'. One of his creditors even wrote to him shortly before his death, saying 'I hope that you will soon extract yourself from being obliged to me or any other in this way by getting a Fair Lady by the hand that will set you upright'.

The 'bon viveur'

Macdonald's bills show that he purchased extremely large amounts of alcohol, even by the standards of the time. From one wine merchant, he obtained on 21 May 1808 alcoholic drinks at a total cost of £161, including a hogshead (50 gallons) of port-wine, alone costing £52 10s. His order also included 12 dozen bottles of sherry, 6 dozen of Madeira, 4 dozen of claret and 4 gallons of shrub (rum and fruit-juice). This level of expenditure in a single day may have been due to the fact that he would have been 21 in 1808; he might well have been celebrating his majority. The fact that it was purchased at Greenock on the west coast suggests that it was destined for a party at his estate rather than at Edinburgh.

His epicurean tastes are attested by various other bills, such as one for the delivery of dinner and various bottles of wine from Oman's Hotel in St Andrew's Street to his lodgings, and at his death he owed an Edinburgh grocer, Mather Carnegie, £50 14s 10d. It may be in this context of conviviality that a John McG... was owed £2 'to carry him home'.

Macdonald's bills also suggest a love of clothes. He had a tailor in London, John Cameron, who was a major creditor at his death, being owed £49 6s, and a tailor in Edinburgh, William Purves, was due £33 10s 9d. From 1813 to 1814 he also ran up debts with John Christie, 'Breeches Maker' of South St Andrew's Street, Edinburgh. These were for expensive, fashionable items such as white doeskin pantaloons, buckskin gloves, leather vests, 'shammy' (chamois) drawers and cashmere trousers.

His tastes also extended to jewellery and other precious items. From a jeweller in Edinburgh, Marshall and Sons, he was invoiced in 1809-10 for a range of items totalling £89 7s including a double-sided gold seal, a gold watch with a second hand costing £23 2s, 18 tumbler spoons, 18 teaspoons, two silver bottle-stands and a silver bread-basket – all engraved with his crest – and an amethyst brooch. He also owned a 'pleasure boat' which was repaired at Greenock in 1809 for £32 10s 5d.

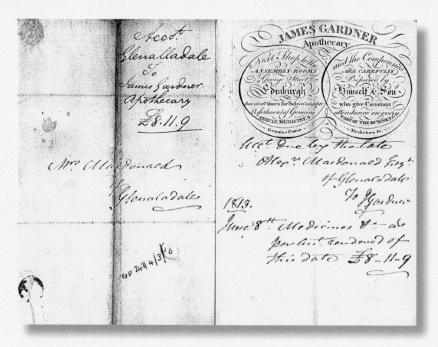

Top: this engraving of Edinburgh shows the tenements at the north end of South Bridge (to left of picture) where Macdonald of Glenaladale lived. They contrast with the splendour of the newly-built Bank of Scotland to the south of the bridge. The picture appeared in Caledonian Sketches, or A Tour through Scotland, by Sir John Carr, published in 1809. Below: a bill from apothecary James Gardner for medicines purchased by Macdonald

Unlike rather grander landowners Macdonald lived in various lodgings and hotels when in Edinburgh as he had no permanent house there. He paid separately on a daily basis for the use of a kitchen and drawing-room at Davidson's Lodgings, situated at 1 North St Andrew's Street. At the time of his premature death he was residing in rented rooms at 5 Princes Street, at the relatively unfashionable south-east end of the street. These lodgings, on the site of what is now the Balmoral Hotel, were in the same block as the tenements of Canal Street and St Ann's Street, referred to in a report for the Town Council of 1817 as 'the meanest and most irregular'.

Macdonald was ill for much of the latter part of 1814. The nature of his illness is not clear, but he employed the services of a Mr E Breham, 'surgeon-dentist' of 2 St David's Street, from whom he ordered bottles of a toothache analgesic; such medicines commonly contained opiates at this date. An 'apothecary' or pharmacist used regularly by Macdonald and still owed money after his death was James Gardner, whose shop was next to the Assembly Rooms in George Street, Edinburgh.

Macdonald's death on 4 January 1815 was recorded in the *Edinburgh Correspondent* of 12 January but it was merely listed without ceremony along with a number of other deceased persons. He had, after all, been living in reduced circumstances. He was buried in Greyfriars Churchyard, Edinburgh on 6 January 1815, a simple inscribed wall-plaque, its inset now lost, marking the position of his grave. As the marble panel at Glenfinnan describes, the Monument was also his memorial.

Macdonald clearly possessed the instincts for show and grand gesture made fashionable in the later eighteenth and early nineteenth centuries and associated with the foppish image of the 'Regency buck', a distinctive character-type of the early Romantic period. In building the Monument, he was certainly attempting to enhance his own reputation in addition to commemorating the Jacobite dead.

Macdonald's grand sense of personal ceremony is underlined by his employment of a personal piper – John MacGillivray – whom he had decked out in fine regalia with a kilt and tartan tunic with frogging. This portrait was drawn by Alexander Kay and published in 1812

The Glenfinnan Monument is sited on a slightly raised area of pebbled and sandy ground, bounded to the east by an area of peaty marsh and to the west by the headwaters of the loch. In some light conditions, the remnants of furrows for early agricultural cultivation can be identified in the nearby grassy areas, particularly when viewed from the hill above.

The idea of using a columnar-based form for a monument goes back to Roman times but Macdonald may well have been influenced by the building of the Nelson Monument on Calton Hill, Edinburgh, begun in 1807. Built mainly of rubble stone, the Glenfinnan tower is a cylindrical structure 18.3 m high and 4 m in external diameter at the base. Although at first glance it seems very simple, it does have a number of distinctive architectural features such as an angled base-course, a doorway of 'Tudor Gothic' style enclosed within a projecting square-headed surround and a crenellated parapet. The tower encloses a spiral stair lit by narrow slit windows, providing access to the open platform on which there stands the statue of a Highlander, added to the Monument in the 1830s.

The rugged character of the masonry of the tower is not how it would have looked originally, when it was finished with a render of mortar and small stones. The rugged exposed stonework we see now is a reflection of the aesthetics of the 1930s, when the original render was removed. From the evidence of an engraving of Glenfinnan of *circa* 1830 (see opposite page), it can be seen that the present faceted perimeter wall is a secondary feature and that originally the Monument was enclosed by a low circular wall.

Engraving of the Monument by Joseph Swan from a painting by John Fleming, c1830. Top left: the 'Tudor Gothic' doorway. Opposite page, top left: the furrows of early agricultural cultivation can be seen close to the Monument

The engraving is also important in showing that abutting the tower to the west was a simple two-storey house or 'bothy', known in early documents as the 'shooting-box'. From its description it was clearly associated with the pastime of shooting game. Interestingly, documents show that Alexander Macdonald purchased a fine pair of double-barrel shotguns and a pair of pistols which were still not paid for at his death, and he can be presumed, like many Highland landowners of the time, to have had a strong interest in fieldsports. From the evidence of contemporary writers, shooting duck across water was a very popular pastime around this period and it is possible that hunters used the low circular wall to hide from their prey. It may also have acted as a breakwater as the water level in the loch varies considerably according to the rainfall.

Documents now in the National Archives of Scotland show that by as early as 1824 the building was in disrepair, and required a range of work including new floors, door and window frames, along with shutters. These sources also indicate that the bothy had two rooms, each with a fireplace, and that these rooms required new lath-and-plasterwork at this time. The staircase needed to be whitewashed and the window frames were to be painted with two coats of white paint.

Whether this work was carried out is not clear, but in the early 1830s another phase of work was begun, removing the bothy and constructing the octagonal perimeter wall. This phase, illustrated in an unpublished anonymous watercolour donated to the National Trust for Scotland (right), was carried out by Angus Macdonald of Glenaladale, the son of the original patron of the Monument. In demolishing the bothy, a functional purpose was removed and the symbolic role of the Monument was enhanced, its visual drama given fuller emphasis by reducing it to a pure columnar form.

Contemporary opinions

The original design of the Monument was described as early as 1824 as like 'a cake house, without even the merit of containing cakes; and with a tower – tower is a profanation of such a word, since the whole building resembles a carpenter's mallet with the handle uppermost.' The writer, John McCulloch, in his book *The Highlands and Western Isles of Scotland*, praised Macdonald for building the monument, but went on to say: 'It is very hard upon poor Scotland, that its money should be thus spent in blotting and deforming its land with such monstrosities; of which it is full from one end to the other; from Nelson's Pillar on the Calton Hill, though that is not the worst …'

A similarly negative view of the building was taken by John Leighton, in *Swan's Views of the Lakes of Scotland* (published in 1834), who wrote: 'It is a sort of tower, with a small house attached, displaying anything but taste in the architect, whoever he was, who unfortunately was employed to erect it; but even as it is, it has a striking effect, when associated with the romantic and unfortunate adventure it commemorates.'

The panels

Built into the perimeter walls in the 1830s were three inscribed cast-iron panels. These record, like the earlier marble panel, that the Monument commemorates Prince Charles Edward Stuart, Alexander Macdonald and his forefathers, and the dead of the Jacobite conflicts. They reflect the intent to transform the tower from private memorial to public commemorative monument, underlined by the parallel texts in Gaelic, Latin and English, whose message is recorded as having been approved of by Scotland's most famous contemporary writer, Sir Walter Scott. The use of parallel texts is reminiscent of the Rosetta Stone – one of the great archaeological discoveries of the age – where hieroglyphs, demotic characters and Greek provided a key to the understanding of a distant culture.

The use of trilingual texts at Glenfinnan, particularly in placing Gaelic on the same footing as Latin and English, was a gesture of some impact in the 1830s, within living memory of the proscription of Highland dress, tartan, and other clan traditions, in the aftermath of the 1745 Rising. Although Gaelic itself was not outlawed, it was strongly associated with the 'treachery' of Highlanders.

The Glenfinnan panels denote a will for Gaelic to be seen as more than a language associated with the unruly Highland clans, but a language also appropriate to heroic sentiments. In this it was reflecting wider cultural changes, of which James Macpherson's *Poems of Ossian*, published in the 1760s, was the single most significant impulse. These tales of Celtic heroism were supposedly translated from Gaelic originals but later proved to be largely Macpherson's own composition. They were internationally renowned. Gaelic was also used on another Highland monument slightly earlier than Glenfinnan – the Well of the Heads beside Loch Oich, which dates from 1812.

The panel with the Gaelic inscription

Gaelic: the voice of the people

Almost all the participants in the event which the Glenfinnan Monument commemorates spoke Gaelic as their first language. At the outset the Rising of 1745 drew much of its military strength from the Gaelic Highlands and Islands and a particular determination from the collision with an increasingly hostile southern culture. The campaign of 'Bonnie Prince Charlie' – this name probably deriving from the Gaelic, *Prionnsa Tearlach* – was one facet of a struggle for the survival and integrity of Gaelic culture and society.

Gaelic songs from this time, when the political voice of the wider population beyond a ruling élite is inaudible, offer rare insights and often vital evidence for the events of 1745-6. First and foremost, they are a call to arms and almost entirely Jacobite in their allegiance. James and Charles are the rightful rulers, Prince Charlie is *Mac an Righ dhlighich* ('Son of the rightful King'), and the campaign a just crusade. The songs recall past bravery and acts of heroism and look to the examples of earlier struggles, particularly in the Civil and Covenanting Wars of the seventeenth century. The songs, passing around readily in oral tradition, were a form of propaganda directed at a wide audience, adoring the Jacobite cause and detesting the Hanoverian, and this function is best represented in the songs of Alexander MacDonald of Moidart, Alasdair Mac Mhaighstir Alasdair. One of his songs is still commonly sung:

O, hì, rì, rì, tha e tighinn…
'O, hì, rì, rì, he is coming,
Hì, rì, rì, the king who we desire,
Let us take up our weapons and battle dress
And the tartan kilt plaided up.'

MacDonald's 'Incitement to the Gaels' is typical of the rousing call to arms and contempt for the Hanoverians:

O fhuair sibh uam bàirlinn, 'us deanaibh dhìth feum,
Us theirgibh 'nur n-èideadh gu dàicheil;
Tha Tearlach a' tighinn le càbhlach garbh treun
A bheir air na beistibh adbhansa.

'O you got from me a warning and make use of it now,
And put on the tartan handsomely.
Prince Charles is coming with a strong mighty fleet
To give battle to the beast.'

Right, top: this Highland targe, decorated with trophies in cast silver, was made in 1740, probably commissioned by James, Duke of Perth, as a gift to Prince Charles (property of Warwick Castle). The one-edged blade (below), made in Germany in 1701 for sale to Scottish Jacobites, bears a portrait of Prince James Francis Stuart and the inscription 'God save King James the 8' (property of Geoffrey Jenkinson)

The statue

The statue, which was added to the tower during the second phase of work, in the 1830s, is the work of a celebrated self-taught Scottish sculptor, John Greenshields (*c*1792-1838). The figure has been widely thought to represent Prince Charles Edward Stuart but no conclusive evidence survives to prove this point. Certainly, the figure is shown wearing the complex form of Highland dress which became popular in the early nineteenth century and was believed typical of a Highland chieftain. The attractive youthfulness of the face and the orientation of the figure away from the loch, as if perhaps awaiting the arrival of his troops, might suggest that it was meant to represent the Prince. The fact that he holds a scroll in his right hand indicates the intention to depict more than a generic Highland character. He also has an insignia on the left side of his chest similar to that shown in some early portraits of Prince Charles.

HIGHLAND CHIEFS,
Dressed in the Stewart and the Gordon Tartans.

Interest in Highland dress was made fashionable by the celebrated writer Sir Walter Scott both before and after the visit of King George IV to Scotland in 1822, which Scott orchestrated as a magnificent pageant, with tartan used copiously for clothing and decoration. The fashion for tartan was also inspired by the publication in 1831 of James Logan's *The Scottish Gael*. This described in detail for the first time, before a better-known volume entitled *Vestiarium Scoticum* was published in 1842, the purported history and complexities of Highland dress before it was outlawed after the 1745 Rising. Much of Logan's information was probably speculative but it was presented in a convincing manner, particularly through the use of engravings showing different forms of Highland dress in detail. Given that there were virtually no other visual sources for Highland dress at this time, it is likely Greenshields would have consulted Logan's book for the detail of his statue. That he did so is strongly suggested by the exact form of the statue's dress and pose – they are virtually identical to the figures in Logan's frontispiece engraving (left).

The architect

Until recently there had been no convincing suggestion regarding the identity of the designer of the Monument. An exciting discovery among documents in the National Archives of Scotland has now made it possible to identify the architect. Among the list of debts of Alexander Macdonald is the sum of £30 9s owed in 1811 to 'James Gillespie, architect'. Undoubtedly, this reference is to one of the foremost architects of the first half of the nineteenth century in Scotland, James Gillespie Graham (1776-1855). He became Gillespie Graham only after his father-in-law died in 1825; documents show he was occasionally referred to as plain James Gillespie well into the 1820s. There is a strong Macdonald connection, as Gillespie Graham had been the Macdonald clan architect on the island of Skye. He had already worked in the vicinity in 1802 when he built Achnacarry Castle for Cameron of Lochiel, Chief of Clan Cameron. He also built Arisaig House, a chapel and a schoolhouse for Alexander Macdonald's chieftain and close friend, Macdonald of Clanranald.

Throughout his career, Gillespie Graham designed over 100 buildings in Scotland, including many well-known country houses such as Duns Castle and Ayton Castle. His St Mary's Cathedral, Edinburgh, built in 1813-14, received great acclaim when completed and really launched Gillespie Graham's career outside the West Highland area.

Above: portrait of James Gillespie Graham by Benjamin Crombie, 1847. Opposite page: entrance front of Gillespie's Armadale Castle, Skye, from the south

It is interesting to compare the Monument with other buildings designed by Gillespie Graham at the same period, as they show many very specific features in common. The architect's designs for Armadale Castle on Skye and Torrisdale Castle in Kintyre, share with the Monument features such as angled plinths, roll-moulding string-courses, slits with monolithic heads and crenellated parapets, as well as other 'Tudor Gothic' details. If the stair turrets at Armadale and Torrisdale are considered separately from the rest of these buildings, it can be seen how similar they are to the tower at Glenfinnan.

According to Macdonald family tradition, the Monument was built by William Miller (1790-1832), a master mason of Fort William.

The Monument in the landscape

The way in which the Monument is situated within the surrounding landscape is entirely in tune with the aesthetic attitudes of the early Romantic period. It conforms to a 'Picturesque' sensibility within the terms defined by contemporary commentators such as William Gilpin. In writing of the Scottish landscape, Gilpin said: 'What makes the first impression on the picturesque eye, are those vast tracts of land, which we meet with entirely in a state of nature.'

Although Glenfinnan was off the main route of Highland tourists in the later eighteenth century, a road was completed between Fort William and Arisaig in 1812 and an inn or 'stage house' was built at Glenfinnan around the same time. The situation of the Monument on low ground, and its dramatic revelation from a turn in the road running around the head of the loch, provide a characteristically Picturesque 'prospect', and it was highlighted from the early nineteenth century as a key site for tourists to visit. Some publications suggest it be viewed from a position – or 'station' – which places it at the centre of the succession of angular mountains by which it is surrounded, and the view from the hill above has been very popular with generations of artists and photographers.

What also provides the Monument with a more profound significance within the aesthetics of the Romantic period is the sense of nostalgia and loss conveyed by its function as a commemorator of the dead. The heralding of the virtues of familial allegiance which it conveys was typical of the period – as conveyed, for example, in Dorothy Wordsworth's journal of her Highland tour with William Wordsworth and Samuel Taylor Coleridge in 1803.

It is also a constant theme in the novels of Sir Walter Scott. This ideal celebrates ancient loyalties and obligations, an image of Scottish history that still has resonance today. The Glenfinnan Monument, with its magnificent surrounding scenery and historic associations, remains a key place for people from all parts of the world with Scottish affiliations.

The making of the landscape

The rugged terrain around Glenfinnan is carved out of hard, crystalline, distinctively banded rocks, belonging to the Moine Supergroup. Original sedimentary layers of sand and silt were laid down around 1,000 million years ago. They were then distorted, recrystallised and partially melted during mountain building processes linked to the movement and collision of tectonic plates that started around 730 million years ago. In the final phases of earth movements, starting around 430 million years ago, these rocks were thrust westwards for up to 100 km over the top of the underlying, even older rocks of the Hebridean basement and the whole region was then uplifted to form the Caledonian mountains. The Moine rocks in this vicinity are particularly distinctive and have been named the Glenfinnan Group. They are cut by veins of pale granite, some with very large crystals, that can be seen in many of the road cuttings.

Reaching up 30 km from the coast at Acharacle, the long, crooked arm of Loch Sheil has all the hallmarks of a deep, narrow sea loch. Though now freshwater, the presence of marine sediments and raised beaches show that once, when sea levels were higher, it was connected to the sea. Now, as then, it still provides a highway to the coast and the regular cruises down the loch from Glenfinnan pier remind us that for most of history this was a major transport route, linking to Loch Eil, whose shores you follow on the road to Fort William.

Flora and fauna

The wildlife around Glenfinnan is an additional attraction for visitors to the Monument. Red deer (opposite) can be seen almost every day. Loch Shiel is renowned as a place for golden eagle spotting and several pairs nest in the surrounding hills. Pipistrelle bats live within the walls of the Visitor Centre, emerging as darkness falls to feed on insects, including the dreaded midge. Other popular sightings are pine martens, wildcats, buzzards, osprey, black-throated divers, herons and swans – the same pair of swans returns every year to nest on the shores of Loch Shiel.

Around the sides of Loch Shiel are some of the broadleaved woodlands typical of the west coast – mostly oak, birch, alder and rowan. The damp conditions make them a haven for mosses and liverworts, which contributed to their designation as a Site of Special Scientific Interest. A major threat to these woodland communities is colonisation by invasive rhododendrons, whose dense, evergreen leaves shade out most of the light and kill anything growing on the woodland floors. In the nineteenth century, rhododendrons were planted in gardens between Glenfinnan and Mallaig, and seeded into the neighbouring woodlands, where they flourished. The Trust has been contributing to a regional effort to eradicate rhododendrons and has been clearing them from the woodland around the river. Further on, towards Arisaig, you will notice many other areas where the rhododendron blanket is being tackled, letting light and air into the mossy carpets below the trees.

Above: (1) heath-spotted orchids; (2) Scotch argus butterfly; (3) six-spotted burnet moth; (4) ragged robin; (5) woodland floor

A monument to the Industrial Revolution

Glenfinnan Viaduct and the West Highland Extension Railway

The Glenfinnan Monument and the Viaduct are public monuments of different generations. These imposing manmade structures add their own historical significance to a landscape that provided an appropriately dramatic natural arena for events of European and international importance.

It is impossible today to recapture the remoteness of the area immediately to the north and west of Fort William as it was in the late nineteenth century. A wilderness of sea and freshwater lochs separated by rocky ridges, and dominated by barren hills, a more unlikely territory for railway-building in the British Isles is hard to imagine. Only the prospect of a government subsidy made it possible to contemplate.

The genesis of the line lay in the promotion in 1884 by the North British Railway company of an ambitious project. This line would have run from Glasgow to Rannoch Moor, down Glencoe to Ballachulish, then crossing Loch Leven to run up the coast of Loch Linnhe to Fort William. There it would have split in two, the main line running up the Great Glen to Inverness, and the other diverging to the west, to Roshven, on the coast south of Lochailort. The Bill for this railway was defeated owing to the opposition of the Caledonian and Highland railways, and of landowners on the route to Roshven, who saw their sporting estates being badly affected. The North British returned to the fray in 1887 with a proposal for the West Highland Railway, which no longer included the route via Ballachulish, and the lines north-east and north-west of Fort William. This Bill was passed.

The opening in 1894 of the section from Craigendoran to Fort William was the springboard for a further extension of railway communication in the western Highlands. The Invergarry and Fort Augustus Railway was built as the first part of a proposed second attempt to reach Inverness, and a new line to the north-west was promoted, this time to Mallaig, opposite Skye. Its construction was made possible because the government was concerned about depopulation and rural poverty in the western Highlands. The North British was offered a guaranteed dividend on part of the capital needed to build the line, which received its Act in 1894.

The terrain en route was easy at first, but beyond the west end of Loch Eil became increasingly difficult. The first short concrete viaduct in Scotland – the Falls of Cruachan Viaduct – had been built in the late 1870s to carry a railway along the north side of Loch Awe. It was constructed with concrete arch rings and masonry spandrels, as was the larger viaduct built in the 1880s on the Killin Railway. On the West Highland Railway similar conditions were encountered at Loch Lomond, and the Creag an Arnain Viaduct was built in a similar way to the pioneering pair. Elsewhere on the West Highland line, however, the viaducts were built with steel trusses on masonry piers.

The contractors who won the tender for the Mallaig line, known officially as the West Highland Extension Railway, were Robert McAlpine and Sons, a firm already well-versed in mass concrete construction. Though the terrain through which much of the line passed was difficult, the long sea lochs allowed supplies to be brought from Glasgow by sea. McAlpine's reckoned that it would be simpler and cheaper to build viaducts and bridges from concrete made using stone removed from the cuttings and tunnels on the line, rather than bringing steel girders up from the south. The mixture they used was one part of Portland cement to four of aggregate, made by crushing the local stone. They found it difficult to recruit navvies, as there was at the time plenty of work in the Lowlands. Despite this, they completed the contract within the time allowed.

Below: the Glenfinnan railway viaduct under construction in the 1890s. Opposite page: North British Railway route map (top) and Fort William to Mallaig timetable – archive items of the 1920s

Glenfinnan Station Museum
A regular train service linking Glasgow, Fort William and Mallaig, with steam engines in summer, still calls at Glenfinnan. The station retains the chalet-style buildings, signal box and mountainside garden, all built at the beginning of the twentieth century and typical of the West Highland line in its heyday. The main station buildings have been restored as a railway museum and interpretive centre, featuring the history of the line from 1889 to the present day. The museum is open from June to September, daily 9.30 to 4.30, or at other times by appointment. For more information telephone 01397 722295.

Glenfinnan Viaduct is the longest structure on the line, and impressive by any standards. It is on a 240-metre curve, the sharpest on any Scottish viaduct, and at its maximum height is 30 metres above the stream it crosses. The arches are all of 50 ft (15 m) span, a standard on the line. It is absolutely plain, with no ornament at all. The structure has an outer skin of concrete made with reasonably fine aggregate, and the interior is filled with larger pieces of stone – known as 'plums' – embedded in the finer material. There is a tradition that a horse and cart fell into one of the hollow piers and that they were buried in concrete rather than recovered. However, recent penetrative radar scans have revealed these skeletal remains not at Glenfinnan, but in the nearby Loch nan Uamh Viaduct .

Though there was undoubtedly a good engineering reason for a viaduct at this point on the line, the way in which it curves round the head of Loch Shiel, affording passengers excellent views of the loch and of the Glenfinnan Monument, leads one to suspect that the engineers, Simpson and Wilson, had an eye to dramatic effect. The tourists were already flocking to the main West Highland line, so the even more spectacular Mallaig line was bound to be equally popular. The relationship with the Monument was of a piece with the Victorian romance with the Jacobites, and especially with Prince Charles Edward Stuart, but it is a two-way relationship. If the viaduct is a fine place from which to view the Monument in its landscape setting, so the Monument is the best place from which to view the viaduct, which is awe-inspiring, with its streaked, still raw-looking, unapologetic grey concrete standing out against the browns and greens of the hills of Lochaber.

The Glenfinnan Viaduct provides a spectacular setting for film makers. It is used most famously in several of the Harry Potter *films, whose 'Hogwarts Express' is in reality the steam locomotive named 'Olton Hall', seen here in its fictional guise as it crosses the viaduct. The engine was built at Swindon in 1937 and designed for the Great Western Railway by Charles Collett. The viaduct has also featured in the film* Charlotte Gray *and the television series* Monarch of the Glen

The Jacobite Trail

Now you have visited the Glenfinnan Monument, why not enjoy the other National Trust for Scotland sites with Jacobite associations?

Killiecrankie
3 miles north of Pitlochry, Perthshire
The first shots in the Jacobite cause were fired in July 1689 at the Battle of Killiecrankie. The Highland army was victorious here over the troops of King William, but their leader, John Graham of Claverhouse ('Bonnie Dundee') was fatally wounded. The 'Soldier's Leap' marks the spot where a fleeing government soldier made a spectacular leap across the beautiful gorge.
Tel 0844 493 2194

Dunkeld
15 miles north of Perth
After their victory at Killiecrankie, the Highlanders took on the Covenanting Cameronians who held Dunkeld. Much of the town was razed to the ground during the battle, and most of the present buildings date from the reconstruction after 1689. The Trust has restored many houses, including its intriguing Ell Shop.
Tel 0844 493 2192

Culloden
5 miles east of Inverness
The evocative Culloden Moor was the scene of the defeat of Prince Charles Edward Stuart's troops on 16 April 1746 – a bitter conclusion to the campaign that began at Glenfinnan and the end of Jacobite hopes of restoring the exiled Stuart dynasty to the throne. The story is excitingly told in the Trust's new Visitor Centre.
Tel 0844 493 2159

Glencoe
17 miles south of Fort William
The spectacular mountain landscape here witnessed the massacre of the MacDonalds of Glencoe in 1692 – ordered by the government of William and Mary as part of their attempt to subdue the Jacobite clans after the rising of 1689. Vivid interpretation of this and the natural history of the glen can be found at the Trust's award-winning eco-friendly Visitor Centre.
Tel 0844 493 2222

Further reading

I G Brown and H Cheape, *Witness to Rebellion. John Maclean's Journey of the Forty-Five and the Penicuik Drawings*, Tuckwell Press/National Library of Scotland, Edinburgh, 1996.

N M Cameron, 'A Romantic Folly to Romantic folly: the Glenfinnan Monument reassessed', in *Proceedings of the Society of Antiquaries of Scotland*, Vol 129 (1999), 887-907.

H Cheape, 'The Culture and Material Culture of Jacobitism', in M Lynch (ed), *Jacobitism and the '45*, The Historical Association, London, 1995, 32-48.

E Corp, *The King over the Water: portraits of the Stuarts in exile after 1689*, National Galleries of Scotland, Edinburgh, 2001.

C Duffy, *The '45: Bonnie Prince Charlie and the untold story of the Jacobite Rising*, Cassell, London, 2003.

J Holloway and L Errington, *The Discovery of Scotland: the appreciation of Scottish scenery through two centuries of painting*, HMSO, Edinburgh, 1978.

F McLynn, *Bonnie Prince Charlie: Prince Charles Edward Stuart*, Vintage, London, 2003.

R K Marshall, *Bonnie Prince Charlie*, HMSO, Edinburgh, 1988

R Nicholson, *Bonnie Prince Charlie and the Making of a Myth: a study in portraiture, 1720-1892*, Associated University Presses, London, 2002.

M Pittock, *The Invention of Scotland: the Stuart myth and the Scottish identity*, Routledge, London, 1991.

R Sharp, *The Engraved Record of the Jacobite Movement*, Scolar Press, Aldershot, 1996.

J Thomas, *The West Highland Railway*, David & Charles, Newton Abbot, 1960.

Access for all

The National Trust for Scotland welcomes disabled visitors. The following facilities are available at Glenfinnan:

- Designated parking spaces adjacent to Visitor Centre
- Good view of monument from Visitor Centre
- Accessible toilet
- Manual wheelchair
- Exhibition, snack-bar and shop accessible
- Commentary with induction loop in Visitor Centre

the National Trust
for Scotland

a place for everyone

The National Trust for Scotland is Scotland's leading conservation organisation. It is not a government department, but a charity supported by its membership of over 300,000.

The Trust was founded in 1931 by a small group of Scots concerned at the growing threat to the country's natural and built heritage. Now, it is an influential body with more than a hundred diverse properties. Its remit, set out in various Acts of Parliament, is to promote the care and conservation of the Scottish landscape and historic buildings while providing access for the public to enjoy them.

Over 76,000 hectares (187,000 acres) of beautiful and dramatic countryside are in the Trust's care, as are over 50 buildings of historical, architectural and social importance. The future of this heritage depends on our ability to meet ever-increasing financial demands. We can do this only with the help of our membership. Please support our valuable work by becoming a member, making a donation or arranging a legacy.

Join the Trust today

Members of the Trust can visit properties FREE of charge. For an annual subscription you have access to over 100 attractions across Scotland and to National Trust properties in England, Wales and Northern Ireland as well. By joining the Trust you can:

- help us to conserve Scotland's heritage now and for the future
- enjoy a great day out
- receive our member magazine three times a year
- receive the definitive annual guide to the Trust's properties
- join a Members' Centre to enjoy talks and outings.

Now, you can join via the Trust's Outdoors Membership and rest assured that your subscription will directly benefit our work outdoors. Extra benefits include free parking at any of our sites with 'pay and display' charges.

Join at any property, or contact the Membership Department on 0844 493 2100, email membership@nts.org.uk

Make a difference

You can also volunteer your time and skills on properties throughout Scotland:

- **Inside our historic buildings and gardens**, many of which could not open to visitors without the support of our volunteers. For more information visit www.nts.org.uk/volunteering
- **NTS Thistle Camps** (and Trailblazer Camps for 16-18 year olds) are residential working holidays covering activities such as gardening, woodland management, archaeological digs and footpath work. Find out more at www.thistlecamps.org.uk
- **Local Conservation Volunteers** groups work on weekend or day projects on countryside properties.
- **Members' Centres** throughout Scotland support the Trust with local conservation work, fundraising, recruitment and guiding at properties. Find out more at www.nts.org.uk or email memberscentres@nts.org.uk

Find out more about volunteering for the Trust at www.nts.org.uk/volunteering

Holidays and cruises

The Trust has a wide choice of self-catering holiday accommodation all over Scotland, ranging from luxury apartments in stately homes to croft houses in the Highlands and lighthouse cottages in remote locations. The Trust also organises a programme of imaginatively themed cruises to remote parts of Scotland and international destinations of particular cultural, historic and conservation interest. For more information tel 0844 493 2108 or visit www.ntsholidays.com

Events at Trust properties

Many of our visitor attractions run special events through the summer season and in the run-up to Christmas. For further information on Trust events, visit www.nts.org.uk

Hospitality

If you are looking for a venue for a special event, whether a wedding, dinner, private party or corporate function, consider the venues offered by the Trust. For a copy of our hospitality brochure, tel 0844 493 2111, or visit www.nts.hospitality.org.uk

The National Trust for Scotland for Places of Historic Interest or Natural Beauty is a charity registered in Scotland, Charity Number SC 007410

Acknowledgements

Authors
Neil Cameron (principal text, on Monument, patron and architect)
Hugh Cheape (Jacobite history and Gaelic culture)
Edward Corp (portraits of the Prince)
John R Hume (Glenfinnan Viaduct)

Edited by Hilary Horrocks

Photography by Mike Bolam
Forth Photography, pages 11, 15, 31

We are very grateful to the following for permission to reproduce images:
Blair Castle, Perthshire for Tullibardine p 12, Murray p 15; Donald Cameron of Lochiel for portrait p 11;
Château de Serrant, France (www.chateau-serrant.net) for painting top p 11, portrait 6 p 20; Christie's
for portrait 7 p 20; CMC Associates/West Highland Railway Archive, West Highland Museum for p 42;
Edinburgh City Libraries and Information Services for 'wanted' poster p 9, engravings pp 32 & 35;
MacBean Collection, University of Aberdeen, for engraving top p 12; National Archives of Scotland
for bills pp 23/24; Trustees of the National Galleries of Scotland for portrait front cover, Baptism p 7,
portrait p 17, portraits 1, 3, 5 pp 18/19; Trustees of the National Library of Scotland for map inside front
cover (EMS.s.91), Prestonpans engraving p 15 (on loan to Scottish National Portrait Gallery), engraving
p 24; Trustees of the National Museums of Scotland for letter p 10, piper p 25, engraving p 27; National
Portrait Gallery, London for portrait p 6, portrait 2 p 18; National Railway Museum/Science & Society
Picture Library for p 43; NTS Photo Library for glass p 6, ship images pp 8/9, plaque p 16, watercolour p
28; The Royal Collection © Her Majesty the Queen for painting p 16; Royal Commission on the Ancient
and Historic Monuments of Scotland © Crown Copyright for pp 13 (The Iain Thornber Collection) & 34;
Stanford Hall, Leicestershire (www.standfordhall.co.uk) for portrait 9 p 21.

Many thanks also to:
John Barnes (Glenfinnan Station Museum), Neil Cameron, Hugh Cheape and Edward Corp for help
with sourcing archive images; Peter Burman, Jill Harden, Richard Luxmoore, David Stephenson (British
Geological Survey), Lyn Turner and Rudy Vandecappelle for advice on text.

Designed by Weesleekit, Moffat, Scotland www.weesleekit.co.uk

Printed in Scotland by Stewarts of Edinburgh

© 2009, The National Trust for Scotland, 28 Charlotte Square, Edinburgh EH2 4ET

ISBN 0 901625 85 X

Glenfinnan Monument,

Glenfinnan, Highland, PH37 4LT
Tel 0844 493 2221

Scottish Natural Heritage
All of nature for all of Scotland

The National Trust for Scotland gratefully acknowledges funding from
Scottish Natural Heritage towards rhododendron clearance and the
installation of visitor counting equipment at Glenfinnan.